# Know Your
# Bible
## for Kids

*Noah's Ark*

# Know Your
# Bible
## for Kids
### *Noah's Ark*

By Ed Strauss
*Illustrated by David Miles*

BARBOUR BOOKS
An Imprint of Barbour Publishing, Inc.

# Contents

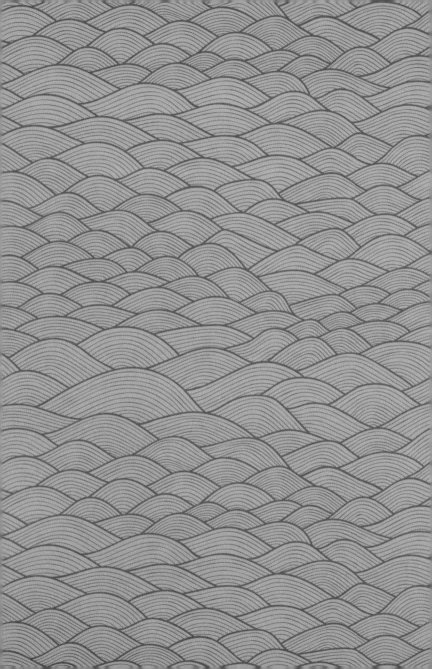

# Introduction:
## Noah—A One-of-a-Kind Hero

Welcome to *Know Your Bible for Kids: Noah's Ark!*
There's something about the story of Noah and the ark
that thrills everyone from kids your age to grandparents.
Very young kids like all the pictures of cute animals.
They enjoy shouting out the names of the creatures they
know. But the story of Noah is much more than a tale of
a boat full of furry friends.

This is an amazing story about a time the world
came to an end. It's an epic adventure about a man who
saved all living creatures from being wiped out. No other
person in the Bible did anything near as fantastic—
until Jesus came along and saved us from our sins. Yes,
Abraham believed God and traveled to a strange land.
Moses did miracles and led the Israelites out of Egypt.
Gideon defeated a huge army of Midianites with only
300 men. But only Noah kept all life on earth from being
destroyed. He was a fantastic hero!

You might have questions about Noah and the ark.
You may even wonder if the Flood really happened or
whether it's just a story. Yes, it really happened. Noah
was a real person. He really built the ark. And the great
Flood—the worldwide Deluge—really did wipe out all
life on land.

Christians who are scientists have studied the
creation of the world and the Flood. They call their
studies Creation Science. And as they looked closely

at the details about Noah, they learned some amazing things. For example, you may or may not like math, but math really helps to understand Noah's story. The Bible gives people's ages and dates and measurements, and when we study these numbers, we see how real Noah's story is.

Noah's Flood is often called the *Deluge* (pronounced day-LOOZH). A deluge is an enormous flood that drowns everything in sight.

Christians have different ideas about Creation and the Flood. Those who believe that the days of Creation in Genesis were each 24 hours long say that the earth is only 6,000 to 10,000 years old. Since they believe that the earth is young, they're called Young Earth Creationists. They say that dinosaurs and people were running around together before the Flood. (The *people* were doing most of the running.) They also believe that the waters of the Flood covered the entire planet—not just part of it.

Other Christians say that God created the world 4.5 billion years ago. Since they believe that the earth is very old, they're called Old Earth Creationists. They think that dinosaurs died out long before Noah's day and that there were just modern animals living then. They believe that Noah built an ark, and that the Flood was very big, but they don't think it drowned the entire planet.

In this book, we tell the story of Noah from a Young Earth viewpoint. But no matter how old you think the earth is, or how big you think the Flood was, the basic facts about Noah and the ark are the same.

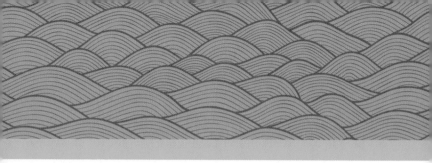

# 1.
# What Was Noah's World Like?

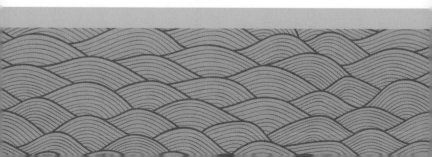

# God Creates a Perfect Planet

When God created the universe, He created the best possible planet for us. "He is God. He formed the earth and made it. . . . He didn't create it to be empty. Instead, he formed it for people to live on" (Isaiah 45:18 NIRV). When He put the final touches on the earth, it was absolutely perfect. "God saw all that he had made, and it was very good" (Genesis 1:31 NIV).

Unfortunately, people have done much to wreck this world since then. They have cut down great forests and filled the world with cities and garbage. They have polluted the water and the air. This world isn't as wonderful as it once was. But it's still very beautiful in places.

Before the Flood, there weren't any gigantic mountain ranges like the Rockies or the Himalayas. Instead of mountains, there were just lots of high hills.

Right from the beginning, there were

Some of the most awesome spots in the world today are:

- the redwood forests in California
- the Grand Canyon in Arizona
- the Arches National Park in Utah
- the Iguazu Waterfalls in Brazil
- the rock towers of the Li River in China

seasons (Genesis 1:14 NKJV). There was winter and summer, spring and fall. But the climate was much milder than today. Winters weren't so cold and summers weren't so hot.

Another big difference was that there weren't seven continents. Genesis 1:9 (NKJV) tells us God said, "Let the waters under the heavens be gathered together into one place, and let the dry land appear." It says that the oceans were gathered together "into *one* place." Many Christians believe that this also means there was just *one* superhuge continent in one place.

Today there are seven continents:

- North America
- South America
- Europe
- Asia
- Africa
- Australia
- Antarctica

# Death Enters the World

The world was perfect until Adam and Eve disobeyed God. When they fell into sin, all the plants and animals were ruined, too. The earth itself was cursed. God told Adam, "Because of what you have done, the ground will be under a curse. You will have to work hard all your life to make it produce enough food for you. It will produce weeds and thorns" (Genesis 3:17–18 GNT).

When his first son was born, Lamech named him *Noah*, which means "relief" or "comfort." He said, "May he bring us relief from our work and the painful labor of farming this ground that the LORD has cursed" (Genesis 5:29 NLT).

Adam and Eve had enjoyed an easy life in the Garden of Eden. It was filled with fruit trees, so for every meal they only had to pick food off the trees. But after they left paradise, they had to work hard for what they ate and everything else.

The apostle Paul wrote, "All creation was [put under] God's curse. But with eager hope, the creation looks forward to. . .glorious freedom from death and decay" (Romans 8:20–21 NLT). The world is not free from death and decay right now. People, animals, and plants suffer diseases, they grow old, and they die. This is all part of the curse.

Many Christians believe that there was no death *at all* in the world before Adam and Eve sinned. No animals hunted and killed other animals for food. If an animal fell and was badly injured, it would soon heal. Something that was living *couldn't* die. If that's the way things were, the world was a very wonderful place.

# Dinosaurs and Dragons

Long ago, before the Flood, great monsters called dinosaurs lived on the earth. And God created them all—the dinosaurs on the land and the dinosaurs in the seas. "God created the great creatures of the ocean. . . . [and] God said, 'Let the land produce all kinds of living creatures'" (Genesis 1:21, 24 NIrv).

Most dinosaurs were wiped out in the Deluge. But Noah took two of every dinosaur on the ark and some of them survived. There were still a few dinosaurs around in Job's day. God told Job, "Look at Behemoth. It is a huge animal. . . . Look at the strength it has in its hips! What power it has in the muscles of its stomach! Its tail sways back and forth like a cedar tree. . . . Its bones are like tubes made out of bronze. Its legs are like rods made out of iron" (Job 40:15–18 NIrv). Many Christians think that Behemoth was a giant land dinosaur like Apatosaurus. It has a tail as thick as a cedar tree!

There was also a terrifying water monster called Leviathan in

Can animals breathe fire? Well, the bombardier beetle produces two chemicals in its body. When it's in danger, the chemicals mix. They make a boiling hot spray that shoots out and burns the creature attacking it.

Job's day. God told him, "The tremendous strength in Leviathan's neck strikes terror wherever it goes. Its flesh is hard and firm and cannot be penetrated. . . . When it rises, the mighty are afraid, gripped by terror. No sword can stop it, no spear, dart, or javelin" (Job 41:22–23, 25–26 NLT).

Leviathan even breathed fire—just like a dragon! In fact, that's likely where the stories of dragons came from. "Flames stream from its mouth; sparks of fire shoot out. . . . Its breath sets coals ablaze, and flames dart from its mouth" (Job 41:19, 21 NIV).

Did people and dinosaurs live together before the Flood? It seems that they did.

# Rain in the Ancient World

Many Christians believe that in Noah's day the whole world had a warm, tropical climate. That is possible, but we don't know for sure. Remember, after Adam and Eve sinned, the entire world came under the curse. So the weather wasn't perfect anymore.

Some people think that it never rained before the Flood, because the Bible says: "When the LORD God made the earth and the heavens, neither wild plants nor grains were growing on the earth. For the LORD God had not yet sent rain to water the earth, and there were no people to cultivate the soil. Instead, springs came up from the ground and watered all the land" (Genesis 2:4–6 NLT).

But all this is saying is that it hadn't rained yet on Day 1 when God created the earth. This was *before* God created plants on Day 3 and *before* He created people on Day 6. But after God created plants and people, it most likely did rain. Wherever there is water and sunshine to heat it, the water cycle happens. Here's how it works:

- Water evaporates and rises as water vapor.
- Water vapor condenses (globs) around dust and pollen.
- Water falls as rain; then the cycle begins again.

Job tells us that God set up this cycle: "He makes

mist rise from the water. Then it falls as rain into the streams" (Job 36:27 NIrv).

However, the rain that fell during the Deluge was very heavy and caused great destruction. There had never ever been a rainstorm like *that* on earth.

# Why People Lived So Long

Before the Flood, people lived for centuries:

- Adam lived 930 years.
- Seth lived 912 years.
- Jared lived 962 years.
- Methuselah lived 969 years.
- Lamech lived 777 years.

Why did people live so long back then? Well, earth is a giant magnet. It's surrounded by a magnetic field. In the past, this magnetism was stronger and stopped most harmful rays of the sun from reaching the earth. These rays couldn't harm people's bodies, so they didn't grow old so quickly.

Some Christians believe there was a "water canopy" around the earth (Genesis 1:6–7). This layer of water also shielded the earth. Like plastic covering a greenhouse, it kept in heat and made the whole earth warm. Then all that water fell as rain during the Flood—and the earth's magnetic field grew weak. That could be why we don't live so long anymore.

But Christian scientists say that if the water canopy had been more than a few inches thick, it would have heated earth too much. The world would have become so hot that no life could have survived. So there must have been just a *tiny* bit of water in the canopy. This was far too little water to flood the world or to shield it from harmful rays.

So probably the main reason that people lived so long before the Flood was because Adam and Eve had perfect bodies. And even though mankind had fallen, their bodies were still very, very healthy.

# How Did People Live?

In Noah's day, most people were farmers. According to Genesis 2:5, God planned for mankind to "work the ground" (NIV) and "cultivate the soil" (NLT) from the start. God told Adam that he would "work hard. . .to get food from the ground" (Genesis 3:17 NIrV). Noah was known as "a man of the soil" (Genesis 9:20 NIV).

But quite a few people also lived in cities. Adam and Eve's son, Cain, built the first city (Genesis 4:17). He called it "Enoch" after the name of his son. It was probably just a group of houses made of mud bricks. After a few centuries, some cities probably got pretty big.

What did they eat? People grew grain, ground the grain into flour, and baked bread. God told Adam, "In the sweat of your face you shall eat bread" (Genesis 3:19 NKJV). They also gathered wild fruits, vegetables, herbs, and spices—the "plants from the field" (Genesis 3:18 NIrV). Some farmers grew grapes and made wine. Noah did (Genesis 9:20–21).

Some people lived in tents and raised cattle (Genesis 4:20). They

God had told people to eat only plants (Genesis 1:29), but people were disobedient to God before the Flood. So many probably killed sheep and cattle and ate their meat.

drank the milk and made butter and cheese out of the cream. Others raised sheep for wool, wove cloth on looms, and made clothing.

People back then had many iron and bronze tools. Hundreds of years before Noah's day, "Tubal-Cain. . . made all kinds of tools out of bronze and iron" (Genesis 4:22 NIrV). This means that they mined iron, copper, and tin and melted them so that they could make tools out of them. Since "the earth was filled with violence" (Genesis 6:11 NKJV), they probably also made many weapons.

They also invented musical instruments like the harp and flute (Genesis 4:21). They then played happy music at their "banquets and parties and weddings" (Matthew 24:38 NLT).

# Sin and Violence Fill the World

When people increased on the earth, their wickedness increased, too. They became very corrupt. To be *corrupt* means to do dishonest, mean things. They robbed and hurt and killed others. They made the poor work like slaves. "God saw that the earth had become corrupt and was filled with violence. God observed all this corruption in the world, for everyone on earth was corrupt" (Genesis 6:11–12 NLT).

People who lived before the Flood had strong bodies *and* smart minds. They might have been simple farmers with simple tools, but they likely invented many new things. When people live hundreds of years, they have time to think a lot.

People did evil things because their hearts were filled with evil thoughts. "When the LORD saw how wicked everyone on earth was and how evil their thoughts were all the time, he was sorry that he had ever made them and put them on the earth" (Genesis 6:5–6 GNT).

God has always been so good to mankind. As the apostle Paul said many years after the Flood, "He has shown kindness by giving you rain from heaven. He gives you crops in their seasons. He provides you with plenty of food. He fills your hearts with joy" (Acts 14:17 NIrV). The people in Noah's day were blessed with God's goodness, too. But they weren't thankful. They were filled with hatred, jealousy, and greed, and they turned from God to idols.

# Sons of God and Giants

Something else very strange was happening just before the Deluge. "The Nephilim were on the earth in those days. That was when the sons of God went to the daughters of human beings. Children were born to them. The Nephilim were famous heroes who lived long ago." (Genesis 6:4 NIrV).

Besides being famous, who were the Nephilim (pronounced NEF-il-im)? Another translation says, "There were giants on the earth in those days" (NKJV). So the Nephilim were giants! And where did these *giants* come from? Well, that's where things get even stranger.

Some Christians believe that "the sons of God" were fallen angels. They think this because angels are called "sons of God" other places in the Bible. Job 1:6 (NIV) says, "One day the

These giants lived after the Flood:

- Ahiman, Sheshai, and Talmai (Numbers 13:22, 33)
- Og (Deuteronomy 3:11)
- Goliath (1 Samuel 17:4)
- Ishbi-Benob (2 Samuel 21:15–17)
- Lahmi, Goliath's brother (1 Chronicles 20:5)
- Saph (2 Samuel 21:18)

angels came to present themselves before the LORD." The Bible was originally written in Hebrew, and the Hebrew words in this verse say "sons of God."

Angels are *not* supposed to have children with humans. That was disobeying God. Of course they had unusual children! But maybe that's *not* what happened after all.

There are other Christians who think that these "sons of God" were men. Maybe they were smart scientists who had found ways to change their bodies and make themselves into super men. Scientists today have already changed animals and plants. If this is what happened back then, that explains why the Nephilim were mighty men.

# God Decides to Judge the World

God had had enough of all the evil things that were happening. So He said, "I will wipe from the face of the earth the human race I have created—and with them the animals, the birds and the creatures that move along the ground—for I regret that I have made them" (Genesis 6:7 NIV).

There was just one righteous man hidden away in a corner of the world. His name was Noah. "But Noah found favor in the eyes of the LORD. . . . Noah was a righteous man, blameless among the people of his time, and he walked faithfully with God" (Genesis 6:8–9 NIV).

Noah was just a simple farmer—like his father Lamech—but he loved and obeyed God.

Then the Lord said, "My Spirit will not struggle with human beings forever. They will have only 120 years to live" (Genesis 6:3 NIrV). Why did God hold off judging the world for 120 years? Because He had decided to save Noah and some of all the animals. To do this, Noah would have to

Noah's parents worked very hard at farming (Genesis 5:29), so when Noah was growing up, he didn't have an easy time. But he loved God and was thankful anyway, so God was able to use him mightily.

build a giant ship. It needed to be *so* big that it would take him 120 years to build.

Noah lived a very long time. He was 600 years old when he built the ark, and he died at the ripe old age of 950!

# 2.

# How Did Noah Build the Ark?

# Noah Gets Set Up

God gave Noah all the details of exactly how to build the ark. It needed to be "450 feet long, 75 feet wide, and 45 feet high" (Genesis 6:15 NLT). It had to be very strong to not break apart in the coming storm. Also, Noah had to build thousands of cages inside the ark. He needed to know from the beginning exactly what design worked best. He couldn't make major changes after he was half done.

In Noah's day, people built many small ships for travel on the ocean. They also built lots of boats for fishing on the lakes and rivers. But no one had ever built anything *this* monstrously big and strong and complicated before.

God told Noah to build the ark out of cypress wood (Genesis 6:14). This wood doesn't rot easily, so it was perfect. Noah needed tons and tons of cypress

This is what Noah's busy work camp needed:

- 🐾 a large house with several bedrooms
- 🐾 other smaller houses for hired workers
- 🐾 a blacksmith shed to make and fix tools
- 🐾 sheds and corrals for work animals
- 🐾 a huge garden and orchard to grow food
- 🐾 a stream and a well for water

wood. He probably moved to a cypress forest and set up there. No sense dragging the heavy lumber any farther than he had to.

Noah also needed strong animals to drag and lift the logs. Like many loggers in Asia, he probably used elephants to do this heavy work.

# Methuselah, Money, and Men

This was a monster-sized job! Noah couldn't possibly do it all by himself. He needed workers to help him—at least to do the hardest work in the beginning. For example, sawing down trees is much faster with two workers on a big saw. These workers didn't believe a flood was coming, but they needed jobs. And they didn't work for free. Noah paid them for their work.

Where did Noah get all this money for 120 years? He was working full-time on the ark, so he couldn't earn this money. Very likely, some of his godly relatives supplied the silver and the gold. After all, since people lived for many centuries, they had lots of time to gain wealth.

Methuselah was Noah's grandfather and was likely a godly man. God allowed him to live 969 years, longer than any other person had lived. And he died *just before* the Flood happened. Why

Noah needed lots of money to

- buy many saws, axes, and other tools
- buy extra food for his workers every day
- buy grain and feed for the work animals
- pay the workers' wages

did he die then? "The righteous perish. . .the righteous are taken away to be spared from evil" (Isaiah 57:1 NIV).

Noah's father, Lamech, also believed in God (Genesis 5:28–29), and the Lord took *him* away when he was 777, just *five* years before the Flood swept over the earth. God took the good people to be with Him.

Methuselah was 187 when Lamech was born. Lamech was 182 when Noah was born. Noah was 600 when the Flood happened (Genesis 5:25, 28–29; 7:6). Now, 187 + 182 + 600 = 969, and Methuselah died when he was 969 (5:27). That's the same year the Flood hit!

# Shem, Ham, and Japheth

You may wonder, "What about Noah's three sons, Shem, Ham and Japheth? I thought that *they* helped their father build the ark!"

They *did* when they grew up. But Noah's three sons weren't even born when he started building. "After Noah was 500 years old, he became the father of Shem, Ham and Japheth" (Genesis 5:32 NIRV). It took him 120 years to build the ark (6:3), and he was 600 years old when the Flood came (7:6). So when his oldest son was born, just after Noah was 500, Noah had already been building the ark for over 20 years.

Shem's name is always mentioned first in the Bible, before his other brothers, because he was the oldest. The Bible says, "Two years after the great flood. . .Shem was 100 years old" (Genesis 11:10 NLT). Now, do the math: Noah was 600 when the Flood hit (7:6), so he was 602 when Shem was 100. Therefore, he was 502 when Shem was born.

Noah's other sons were born after Shem. But Ham wasn't the next

Noah's workers were probably relatives. Noah had many younger brothers and sisters (Genesis 5:30). But the sad thing was, they didn't believe a flood was coming, and none of them boarded the ark.

oldest. The Bible tells us that Ham was Noah's "youngest son" (Genesis 9:22, 24 nirv), so Japheth was the middle kid. We don't know how many years after Shem these brothers were born.

Many Christians believe that Shem was the ancestor of the Semites (Arabs and Jews) and of all Asian peoples. Japheth was the father of the Europeans. And Ham was the ancestor of the Africans.

How were such different sons born to the same father and mother? Well, lots of people in America have many different ancestors. Some of their ancestors were Irish, German, Nigerian, Cherokee, or Chinese. Some children in the family look more Irish; others look more Cherokee. Yet they're from the same two parents.

Noah's three sons grew up working on the ark. When all the heaviest work was done and all the paid workers left, Shem, Ham, and Japheth were still there. They along with Noah probably finished the ark alone in the last years.

## The Shape and Size of the Ark

Some little kids' picture books show the ark as a curvy boat, just big enough for a couple of elephants, a pair of monkeys, one giraffe, and. . .that's about it. But the ark was huge! Hundreds and hundreds of elephants could have fit inside it!

God told Noah to make the ark 300 cubits long, 50 cubits wide, and 30 cubits high (Genesis 6:15 NKJV). A "cubit" was the distance from a man's elbow to his fingertips. So that means the ark was:

- 450 feet long
- 75 feet wide
- 45 feet high

The ark wasn't shaped like a modern ship. It was shaped like a huge, huge wooden box. It wasn't built to look beautiful. It just needed to keep people and animals alive.

The first thing Noah did was clear off a flat piece of ground on which to build the ark. Then he chopped down trees and built his own house. He built sheds and corrals for his work camp. He plowed some land and planted a garden and an orchard. Finally he was ready to start building the ark.

Most people thought that Noah was crazy. They made jokes about him. But He believed that God had spoken to him. "It was by faith that Noah built a large boat to save his family from the flood. He obeyed God, who warned him about things that had never happened before. By his faith Noah condemned the rest of the world, and he received the righteousness that comes by faith" (Hebrews 11:7 NLT).

# Building the Ark

Work seemed to go really slow for many years. First Noah and his workers had to fell lots and lots of large trees. Then they had to use hammers and wedges to carefully carve them into long, flat boards and thick beams.

They smeared the bottom beams with pitch. Then they set them in the sun to dry. This pitch wasn't tar made from oil, because there was no oil in the ground yet. This pitch was tree sap, and it hardened and made the bottom of the ark waterproof.

When they had enough beams and boards, they built the bottom floor of the ark. Some people think Noah didn't use nails because they hadn't been invented yet. But the ark wouldn't have held together during such a wild storm without nails. Besides, they had many types of tools back then. Hundreds of years before Noah's day, "Tubal-Cain. . . made all kinds of tools out of bronze and iron" (Genesis 4:22 NIrv). So they probably had nails, too.

Noah probably used cranes. These were tall wooden towers with thick, strong ropes to swing the lumber into place. Where

Why did Noah succeed in his mission? God gave him detailed instructions, and "Noah did everything exactly as God commanded him" (Genesis 6:22 NIrv).

did they get all that rope from? Probably the wives of the workmen wove it.

When the ark was finally completely built, they sealed it with resin from top to bottom, outside and inside, to make it waterproof (Genesis 6:14). Meanwhile, although the world was very wicked, "God waited patiently while Noah was building his boat" (1 Peter 3:20 NLT).

Also, the women probably

- did the gardening
- milked the cows
- made cheese
- ground the grain
- baked bread
- did the cooking

# Rooms in the Ark

God told Noah to build three levels in the ark, saying, "You shall make it with lower, second, and third decks" (Genesis 6:16 NKJV). When Noah built the bottom level of the ark, he divided this deck into many animal pens and cages. The bigger, heavier animals like elephants, hippos, rhinos, and dinosaurs would all go on this deck, so their rooms were large.

Now, the ark was 45 feet high, so perhaps all three levels were 15 feet high each. But maybe not. Maybe the lowest level, where the biggest animals were, had a ceiling 20 feet high, and the two upper levels were each only 12½ feet high. After all, the smaller animals didn't need such a high ceiling.

God gave Noah commonsense plans. The biggest, heaviest animals had to be on the bottom deck of the ark, not the top. Otherwise it might have been unbalanced during the storm.

The middle deck was built above the lowest deck. Medium-sized animals would be on this level. So Noah and his workers built smaller pens for sheep, pigs, cattle, deer, antelope, ostriches, lions, and tigers. And of course, all of the medium-sized dinosaurs like Struthiomimus and Velociraptors were there.

The top deck was built above that. It was where all the small, light animals would be—the rabbits, geese, dogs, raccoons, and all the thousands and thousands of birds, butterflies, bats, bees, and insects. So there were many, many small wooden cages. Very likely Noah's sons spent months—or even years—building birdcages. They became experts at it.

Noah and his sons most likely built their living quarters in the middle of the top deck. We'll have a closer look at their dwelling later.

# The Layout of Each Deck

The Bible doesn't give us the details on how each deck was laid out. But we can make some guesses on how God might have planned it. For example, we know that there were three levels to the ark. We also know that there were cages and pens on every level, because God told Noah to "make rooms in the ark" (Genesis 6:14 NKJV).

We also know that Noah and his sons had to feed and water the animals every day for one year. So a good plan would have been to have the cages in long rows down the length of the ark. It also would have been good to have long hallways for Noah and his sons to walk on, to easily reach all the cages.

Since the ark was 75 feet wide, there could have been three rows of cages on the bottom two levels. That means one row on the left side, a row in the middle, and another row on the right side. There would've been two long hallways between them.

If the wooden beams of the ark's outer walls were 2½ feet thick, then each cage would have been 19 feet wide, and each hallway would have been 6½ feet wide.

$(2½ + 19 + 6½ + 19 + 6½ + 19 + 2½ = 75)$

So the pens and cages could have been a good size. They would have each had plenty of room for the animals to walk around in.

The top deck with all the birds and small animals could have had more than three rows. After all, their cages didn't need to be so big. So they could have had five rows of cages 10 feet wide, with four hallways 5 feet wide.

$(2½ + 10 + 5 + 10 + 5 + 10 + 5 + 10 + 5 + 10 + 2½ = 75)$

# Light, Fresh Air, and Waste

While the ark was swept along on the raging waters, Noah and his family had to be very careful with fire. After all, the entire vessel was made of wood. It was a real fire hazard! They had to cook food and bake bread, but they had a safe oven.

They had to be careful carrying lit lamps around, since the ark was constantly tipping back and forth in the waves. So most lamps would have been fastened to the hallway walls. But they couldn't have lamps everywhere. So was most of the inside of the ark totally dark? It *was* pretty dark, especially the lowest deck. But there was more light on the top deck. God had told Noah, "Leave an 18-inch opening below the roof all the way around the boat" (Genesis 6:16 NLT). Because it was on top of the ship's sides, and the roof covered it, it didn't let in much rain.

Most importantly, this 18-inch window all around the top let in lots of fresh air! The ark would have been *very* smelly with all those thousands and thousands of animals. And think of all the animal waste—both solid and liquid—piling up on the bottom of the ark. So fresh air was very important.

A bit of sunlight—and especially fresh air—needed to reach the decks below. Here's how Noah could have made that happen: instead of building all the hallway floors out of solid boards, he could have made part of them out of latticework. (A "lattice" is many thin boards that crisscross each other.) These lattices would have let light and air pass through to the deck below.

# Food and Water

Noah and his family and all the animals had to live on the ark for over a year. They needed food every day. So God told Noah in the beginning, "Take every kind of food that you will need. Store it away as food for you and them" (Genesis 6:21 NIrV).

This food was mostly grain. Cattle and sheep eat grain. Most birds eat grain. And dry grain is easy to store. So there would have been large grain storage rooms on every deck. Imagine people bringing wagonload after wagonload of grain to Noah's work camp in the last year. That would have cost him lots of money! Noah would have also stored tons of dried grass and straw on the ark.

They boarded the ark seven days early (Genesis 7:1, 4, 10). The Flood began in month 2, day 17 of Noah's 600th year (7:11). They came out of the ark in month 2, day 27 of Noah's 601st year (8:13–16). So how long were they on the ark? For one year and 17 days!

They needed lots of water on the ark, but remember: it rained for 40 days and nights. Water that landed on the roof of the ark could have gone into gutters and pipes that led down into water containers.

Other foods Noah probably stored:

- ❧ dried grapes (raisins)
- ❧ figs and dates
- ❧ nuts and berries
- ❧ honey and cheese

# 3.
# What Kinds of Animals Were on the Ark?

## Clean and Unclean Animals

God told Noah, "Bring a male and a female of every living thing into the ark. They will be kept alive with you. Two of every kind of bird will come to you. Two of every kind of animal will also come to you. And so will two of every kind of creature that moves along the ground" (Genesis 6:19–20 NIrv).

God considered certain kinds of animals "clean" and other kinds of animals "unclean." The "clean" land animals were those that had split hooves that chewed the cud (Leviticus 11:1–7). These included:

- cattle and bison
- deer and antelopes
- sheep and goats
- water buffalo

God especially wanted "clean" animals to multiply on the earth. So He told Noah, "Take seven pairs of every kind of 'clean' animal with you. Take a male and a female of each kind. Take one pair of every kind of animal that is not 'clean.' Take a male and a female of each kind. Also take seven pairs of every kind of bird. Take a male and a female of each kind" (Genesis 7:2–3 NIrv).

However, some kinds of birds were "unclean." (See the list of birds in Leviticus 11:13–19.) Only two of each unclean bird came on the ark. So that means there were only two disgusting vultures on the ship. But seven of every clean bird that existed came on board the ark. Since most birds are "clean," that was a *lot* of birds!

There was another reason there needed to be extra "clean" animals on the ark. After the Flood, Noah sacrificed one of each of them to God as a "burnt offering" (Genesis 8:20).

# Meat-Eating Animals

After Creation, God told people, "I have given you every seed-bearing plant throughout the earth and all the fruit trees for your food. And I have given every green plant as food for all the wild animals. . . everything that has life" (Genesis 1:29–30 NLT). So in the very beginning, both people and animals were vegetarian. (They only ate vegetables and other plants.)

After the Deluge, things changed. God told Noah, "All the animals of the earth. . .I have given them to you for food, just as I have given you grain and vegetables" (Genesis 9:2–3 NLT). That's when God gave people permission to start eating meat.

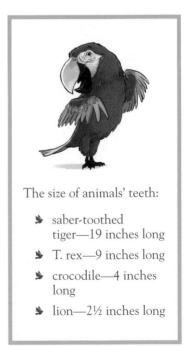

Many Christians think that carnivorous animals *also* only ate plants before the Flood. But the Bible doesn't actually say that. It only says that *people* were vegetarians. Carnivorous animals probably started hunting and eating meat

The size of animals' teeth:

- ➤ saber-toothed tiger—19 inches long
- ➤ T. rex—9 inches long
- ➤ crocodile—4 inches long
- ➤ lion—2½ inches long

right after the curse came. After all, the earth was "full of violence" before the Flood (Genesis 6:11 NIV).

God gave lions such sharp teeth and claws for a reason. And Velociraptors had whole mouthfuls of pointy teeth. And what did anteaters eat until then, if not ants? Also, death entered the world at the curse. So that's probably when hyenas, jackals, and vultures began eating the dead bodies of animals. They're the "garbagemen" of nature.

If there were meat eaters on the ark, then Noah must have killed a whole flock of sheep just before the Flood. Then he would have smoked and dried the meat and stored it on the ark for the carnivores. That's possible. Adam's descendants had been sacrificing sheep ever since leaving the Garden of Eden (Genesis 4:4). And Noah sacrificed hundreds "of every clean animal and of every clean bird" after the Flood (Genesis 8:20 NKJV).

# Size and Weight of Animals

Some animals, like African elephants, are really huge. They're 10 to 13 feet tall at the shoulder and weigh 9,000 to 15,000 pounds. Others, like mice, are small. Some, like ladybugs and ants and flies, are tiny. They weigh practically nothing. But all these creatures, from the greatest dinosaurs to the thousands of different kinds of insects, came on board the ark.

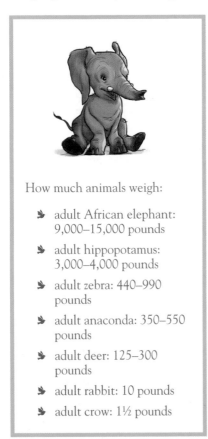

How much animals weigh:

- adult African elephant: 9,000–15,000 pounds
- adult hippopotamus: 3,000–4,000 pounds
- adult zebra: 440–990 pounds
- adult anaconda: 350–550 pounds
- adult deer: 125–300 pounds
- adult rabbit: 10 pounds
- adult crow: 1½ pounds

As we learned already, the heaviest, biggest animals were kept on the lowest deck, down in the basement of the ark. The middle-sized animals were kept on the middle deck.

The bugs were very likely kept on the top deck with the birds—though of course they were separated from them. We don't know if birds ate insects before the Flood, but they probably did. So Noah had to make sure none of the birds escaped from their cages. They would have gone crazy trying to eat all the bugs!

Some animals are huge and weigh a lot. Other animals are tiny and weigh very little. But the *average* animal in the world is the size of a small female sheep—and weighs about 100 pounds. You'll find out soon how this fact tells us some important things.

# Amazing Ark Math

A normal ship, when loaded with passengers and cargo, sinks halfway in the water. Half the ship is below the water, and half sticks above the surface. Since the ark was 45 feet high, *half* its height was exactly 22½ feet.

"The water covered even the highest mountains on the earth, rising more than twenty-two feet above the highest peaks" (Genesis 7:19–20 NLT). The original Hebrew words say the water was "15 cubits" above the mountaintops. And 15 cubits is exactly 22½ feet. The Flood had to be 22½ feet deeper than the highest mountains because that's how far the ark's bottom was below the surface. God didn't want the ark scraping against a mountain top.

Since we know that the ark rode 22½ feet deep, we can figure out how much it weighed. The part of a ship underwater displaces water (pushes it out of the way). And a ship weighs as much as the water it displaces. So when we multiply the ark's length by its width by *half* its height,

A "cube" is a square block, like a sugar cube or a child's playing block. A "cubic foot" of water is 1 foot high, 1 foot wide, and 1 foot long.

we can figure out its weight. Now, 450 feet x 75 feet x 22½ feet = 759,375 cubic feet.

One cubic foot of ocean water weighs about 62.4 pounds. So we know that the ark weighed 47,385,000 pounds. That's about 24,000 tons!

Experts say that the heavy wooden ark and all the food and drinking water stored on it made up about 90 percent of this weight. The animals weighed the other 10 percent. So when we divide 47,385,000 pounds by 10, we see that there were 4,738,500 pounds (2,400 tons) of animals. Now, the average animal weighs 100 pounds. So when we divide 4,738,500 pounds by 100, we see that there were about 47,385 animals on the ark!

But some Bible teachers have counted all the different species of animals in the world, and they've decided that there were probably only 16,000 animals on the ark. What does this mean? It means that, if they are right, the ark wasn't crowded at all. There was plenty of room for *all* the animals—and even room left over.

# Many Kinds of Animals

You may wonder why some people think there were only 16,000 animals on the ark. You may even think there had to be *more* than 47,385 animals. After all, aren't there millions of different species on earth? And God *did* tell Noah, "You are to bring into the ark two of all living creatures, male and female, to keep them alive with you. Two of every kind of bird, of every kind of animal and of every kind of creature" (Genesis 6:19–20 NIV).

Some people think that the original Hebrew word *myin* (translated "kind") means "species." So they think that God was telling Noah to bring "two of every species of bird, of every species of animal, and of every species of creature." Since the ark only carried 2,400 tons of animals, millions of species wouldn't have fit.

But there *weren't* millions of species on earth. A "species" is a group of animals whose males and females can mate and

Zebras and donkeys can mate and produce young called *zonkeys*. So zebras and donkeys belong to the same "kind." Lions and tigers can mate and produce young called *ligers*. So they both belong to the same "kind."

produce babies that can *also* produce babies. There are hundreds of breeds of dogs in the world, but they're all one species. (Dogs are just tame wolves.) A schnauzer can mate with a poodle and produce a snoodle! Also, there are many, many breeds of cats, but they're all one species.

Noah didn't have to take many different kinds of dogs on the ark. He just had to take one male wolf and one female wolf—and from those two wolves came all the dogs on the planet today. The same holds true for many other kinds of animals.

# Dinosaurs aboard the Ark

Christians who believe in Young Earth Creationism say that dinosaurs and people lived together before the Deluge. Christians who believe in Old Earth Creationism say that dinosaurs died out *long* before Noah's day.

Now, if dinosaurs were living in Noah's day, he would have taken two of every kind of them on the ark. After all, God told Noah, "You are to bring into the ark two of all living creatures, male and female, to keep them alive with you" (Genesis 6:19 NIV). But some people ask, "Even though the ark was big, it wasn't *that* big. How could they fit?"

Many dinosaurs, such as T. rex and Brachiosaurus, *were* gigantic when they were full grown. And a 50-foot-tall Ultrasaurus would have been too

How much adult dinosaurs weighed:

- Stegosaurus—6,000 pounds (3 tons)
- Ankylosaurus—13,000 pounds (6½ tons)
- Triceratops—20,000 pounds (10 tons)
- Brachiosaurus—100,000 pounds (50 tons)
- Ultrasaurus—140,000 pounds (70 tons)

huge to fit under a 20-foot ceiling on the bottom deck. And since it weighed 70 tons, it would have been way, *way* too heavy for the ark. It would have crashed right though the floorboards. So God sent *young* dinosaurs onto the ark. They finished growing after the Flood.

There were also oversized prehistoric mammals like Brontotheres, giant ground sloths—and the hugest land mammal of all time, Indricotherium. So God brought only the young of these animals on the ark.

Not all dinosaurs were monstrous. Some were only as big as people, and others were as small as chickens.

# Gathering the Animals

Some people wonder how animals from all different continents got on the ark. But remember: back then the world wasn't divided into seven continents. There was only one superbig mass of land. You can see on a map how South America and Africa fit each other like pieces of a puzzle. They were once joined. They split apart because of the Flood.

So while the land was still joined, the animals could have traveled hundreds or thousands of miles to where Noah was. Even today, huge herds of reindeer migrate. (To migrate means to travel from one area to another.) Sometimes reindeer travel 3,000 miles in one year. Also, every year 1.5 million wildebeest and 300,000 zebra (and many antelope) travel 1,800 miles from Tanzania to Kenya.

So Noah didn't have to chase all the animals and trap them in cages. God simply called them to the ark and they came. "Pairs of 'clean' animals and pairs of animals that

"Even the stork that flies across the sky knows the time of her migration, as do the turtledove, the swallow, and the crane. They all return at the proper time each year" (Jeremiah 8:7 NLT).

were not 'clean' came to Noah. . .and entered the ark" (Genesis 7:8–9 NIrv).

God makes many animals migrate. Salmon live their whole lives out in the ocean, yet when it's time to lay eggs, they return to the very spot on the same river where they were born. Every year, arctic terns fly from the top of the globe to the bottom—and back again. That's 24,000 miles! Even delicate monarch butterflies migrate thousands of miles and know exactly where to go.

# Animals Not on the Ark

Many animals didn't need to go on the ark to survive. Think of all the billions of fish in the ocean. They were mostly fine. Also, whales, killer whales, porpoises, dolphins, seals, and many other kinds of water mammals managed quite well.

Of course, even many fish had a rough time. The waves were wild, and millions of tons of mud were burying animals under the water. Scientists have found fossil fish that were smothered in mud. They were "frozen" as fossils, twisting around, trying to escape.

And many fish, sea creatures, crabs, and microbes living in the ocean had a really wild ride. One minute they were living peacefully in the sea. Then, according to Genesis 7:11, "the fountains of the great deep" (NKJV) broke apart and "all the underground waters erupted from the earth" (NLT). Fish were caught in the spray and shot miles upward.

Experts believe that the water was under such pressure that it shot 20 miles high. Some water flew so high that it escaped into outer space. Others say that some water ended up on the moon. (There's water there, but scientists can't explain how it got there.) So if you think a monkey was the first living creature to go into outer space, you might be mistaken. Lots of small fish and plankton could have gone there first.

Meanwhile, back on earth, the ark was riding out the storm. Many animals that spend a lot of time in water— such as hippos, alligators, penguins, and otters—couldn't have survived for a year in the ocean. They had to come on the ark, too. We don't know whether Noah built them water tanks to soak in or not. He probably did.

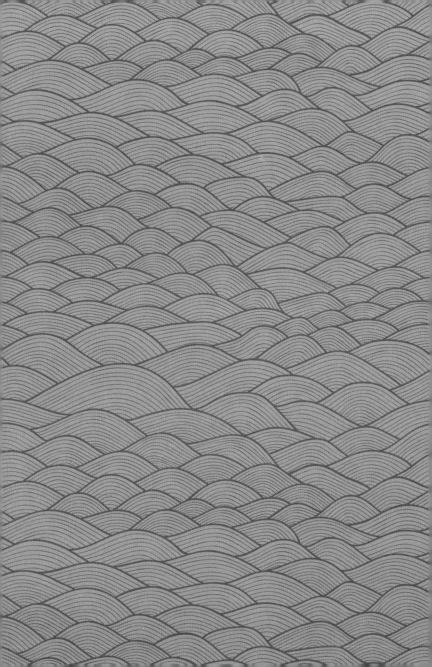

# 4.

# How Did the Flood Happen?

# The Water Canopy

Christians once thought that before the Flood there was a water canopy above the earth. A canopy is a covering "floating" above something—like a covering hanging above a throne. And people believed that a covering of water surrounded earth, high above the atmosphere.

God had said, "'Let there be a firmament in the midst of the waters, and let it divide the waters from the waters.' Thus God made the firmament, and divided the waters which were under the firmament from the waters which were above the firmament; and it was so. And God called the firmament Heaven" (Genesis 1:6–8 NKJV).

Some people thought that the firmament wasn't firm at all. They guessed that God was talking about the air. This is because Genesis 1:20 (NKJV) says, "Let birds fly above the earth across the face of the firmament of the heavens." Since there were oceans beneath the

*Firmament* means something firm or solid. The Hebrew word *raqia* (firmament) comes from the word *raqa*. *Raqa* means "to beat or spread out." Think of metal hammered out into a sheet. Metal is very firm, but it can be made flat.

sky, they thought, that must mean that there was also water above the sky.

What actually was the firmament? These days, most experts think the firmament means the earth's crust. There was water 10 miles below the crust in underground oceans, and there were waters above the crust in the oceans. And the earth's crust was between them.

In June 2014, scientists announced that there are huge amounts of water below the earth's crust. This water is inside rocks 255–410 miles deep. There is as much water still down there as there is in all the oceans of the world.

Then why did God call the firmament "heaven"? Because the Garden of Eden was on earth. The entire world was a paradise. And God walked with people on earth. But that happy time soon ended.

# The Water Canopy Falls

Many scientists believe in evolution. They say that millions of years ago, a large meteorite hit the earth with terrific force. It caused a great earthquake, crushed rocks, and sent tons and tons of dust high into the atmosphere. It started forest fires all around the earth, and this put millions of tons of ashes into the air. Thick black clouds covered the world. The sun couldn't shine through the clouds so the earth became very cold. Most dinosaurs and most plants died out.

They believe they've found proof for this. They discovered an enormous crater near the town of Chicxulub in the Yucatan Peninsula of Mexico. Later they discovered more giant craters.

Here are the largest meteor craters on earth:

- Vredefort (South Africa): 190 miles in diameter
- Sudbury (Canada): 160 miles in diameter
- Chicxulub (Mexico): 110 miles in diameter
- Popigai (Russia): 55 miles in diameter
- Acraman (Australia): 55 miles in diameter

Some Christians said that these craters helped explain the Flood. They said that when the meteors hit, dust and ashes rose high into the atmosphere. The water canopy formed drops around them and fell as rain for 40 days.

Still, there were problems with this idea. First, as we already learned, experts say that if the water canopy had been more than a few inches thick, it would have overheated the planet. No life could have survived. So there must have been just a tiny bit of water in the canopy—nowhere near enough to flood the world.

Also, Genesis 1:16–17 (NKJV) says that God "made the stars. . .to give light on the earth." Yet, if the water canopy had held billions of tons of water, no one could have seen the stars through it. Finally, if there was water floating high above the earth, it would have quickly evaporated into outer space.

# The Earth Cracks Up

A Christian named Walt Brown wrote *In the Beginning: Compelling Evidence for Creation and the Flood.* In his book, he explained how he thought the Flood happened.

In the beginning, there were vast oceans deep beneath the earth's crust. These were "the waters which were under the firmament." They were about 10 miles down. With the heavy crust on top of them, these oceans were under very great pressure. The water also put pressure on the crust above it. The crust was just waiting to burst apart. And one day it did.

"When Noah was 600 years old. . . all the underground waters erupted from the earth, and the rain fell in mighty torrents from the sky" (Genesis 7:11 NLT).

Brown taught that when water shot out from the underground oceans, it broke the earth's crust into big pieces called "plates." Since *hydro* means "water," it's called the hydroplate theory.

If you look at a map of the ocean bottoms, you can see these cracks. You will see what looks like a long zipper down the middle of the Atlantic Ocean. This crack is called the Mid-Atlantic Ridge.

When God was ready to send the Flood, the crust began cracking in a weak spot. Perhaps when all those huge meteorites slammed into the earth, they made the crust crack. The pressure of the water below was so great that this crack grew at lightning speed. In two hours it circled the entire planet, ripping the earth's crust apart. Meanwhile, water was bursting out of the many cracks. It exploded 20 miles up into the air. It kept spraying up for 40 days and fell back to earth as heavy rain.

# The First Forty-Seven Days

Before the Deluge came, God gave Noah and his family a week to get used to living on the ark. "Noah and his sons and his wife and his sons' wives entered the ark. . . . and after the seven days the floodwaters came" (Genesis 7:7, 10 NIV). As soon as the Lord closed the door (7:16), they needed to start feeding and watering the animals. The animals got used to being in the dark in small pens. And Noah's family got used to their chores.

Suddenly, there was a thunderous cracking as the earth ripped apart! The ground shook. Then there was a roar as billions of tons of water burst out. Not long after, heavy rain began crashing on the roof of the ark. And it didn't stop for 40 days and 40 nights.

Noah probably built the ark on high ground. That way, it didn't begin floating right away. It avoided bumping into tons and tons of floating tree trunks and junk at the beginning. But after several days of rain, the Flood finally reached the ark. Then it began to float.

At first, the animals were terrified by the earthquakes, the roaring water, and the pounding rain. They roared and howled and tried to escape. But Noah and his sons had built the pens and cages very strong, and they couldn't get out.

"For forty days the floodwaters grew deeper, covering the ground and lifting the boat high above the earth. . . . Finally, the water covered even the highest mountains on the earth" (Genesis 7:17, 19 NLT). Before the Flood, the mountains weren't that big. They were really only high hills less than a mile tall.

# The Continents Separate

All the earth's crust cracked apart in just a couple of hours. It separated into seven large plates and several smaller ones. But that was only the beginning of the action. Terrific geysers of water roared up between the cracks. They kept pushing the plates farther and farther apart. Soon some plates were moving very fast away from each other.

As all the heavy crust slid across the earth below, it caused earthquakes around the world. And these earthquakes caused many tsunamis on the ocean. (Tsunamis are monster-sized waves.) Soon enormous waves were sweeping around the world. They caused great destruction. All the people who tried to escape in boats and ships were drowned by these monster waves. Only the ark was big enough and built well enough to survive.

These were the biggest tsunamis in modern history:

- Yaeyama, Japan (1771)—262 feet high
- Unzen, Japan (1792)—330 feet high
- Krakatoa, Indonesia (1883)—100 feet high
- Sanriku, Japan (1896)—125 feet high
- Indian Ocean (2004)—100 feet high

At first, many scientists thought that even the ark would have cracked apart in all those gigantic waves. But then they discovered something amazing. The way the ark was built much longer than it was wide meant that it would have simply been driven along with the waves. It wouldn't have broken up.

You may have wondered what that big wooden thing is at the front of the ark, on top. That was like a short wooden "sail." It caught just enough wind to keep the ark pointed forward. Also, there was probably a giant rudder on the back of the ark to keep it steering straight. Ancient Greek and Roman ships were also made that way.

Ark experts learned that the way the ark was built made it impossible to tip over. No matter how far it leaned to one side, it always would bounce back. It couldn't sink. Noah wasn't a master shipbuilder, but God is. He knows everything, and He gave Noah a perfect plan.

# Five Months of High-Speed Sailing

For 40 days, the rain never stopped pounding on the roof of the ark. Noah and his family had gotten used to all the noise. They probably also wondered if it had really been such a good idea to live in the top deck of the ark, just under the roof. Then one day there was a strange silence. The rain stopped!

There was no need for it to keep raining. The entire earth was flooded. Even the highest hills and mountains were covered with water. Remember, they weren't so tall before the Flood.

There was no more rain, but there was still plenty of noise. The Lord sent a mighty wind (Genesis 8:1), so for the next 110 days, waves crashed steadily against the ark. And the earth's crust was still spreading apart,

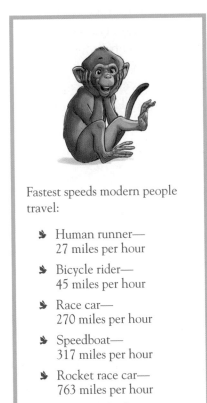

Fastest speeds modern people travel:

- ➴ Human runner—
  27 miles per hour
- ➴ Bicycle rider—
  45 miles per hour
- ➴ Race car—
  270 miles per hour
- ➴ Speedboat—
  317 miles per hour
- ➴ Rocket race car—
  763 miles per hour
- ➴ Airplane (jet)—
  2,193 miles per hour

so there were still earthquakes and tsunamis. But the ark was so well built that it kept on floating.

In fact, it wasn't just "floating." Tsunamis can travel 500 miles per hour across the ocean, so the ark was shooting along at fantastic speed. The ark probably went around the globe a few times—first this way, then that way, then another way.

Meanwhile, terrific forces caused high mountain ranges to be pushed up. These forces also caused the ocean depths to sink deep down. So even though the same amount of water covered the earth, the water began sinking into the depths. The water level began going down. It kept going down for the next 110 days. (We'll see later what caused this.)

# The Ark Lands

One day there was a loud scraping against the bottom of the ship. The ark stopped moving. "At the end of the hundred and fifty days. . .the ark came to rest on the mountains of Ararat" (Genesis 8:3–4 NIV). It might have stopped so suddenly that Noah and his family were thrown off their feet. Or God could have made it set down very gently. But however it happened, it happened.

Noah and his entire family probably ran to the windows and looked out. But they didn't leave the ark. . . not yet. They must have really wanted to leave, but they couldn't. Most of the world was still covered with water. So they sat there for the next seven and a half months. But they weren't without chores to do. They still had to feed and water all the animals every day. They still had to clean out tons of waste every day.

The mountains of Ararat were brand new. They didn't exist before the Flood. We know this because (1) they're so tall, and (2) they sit on a huge lava plateau that was formed by a volcano. When the earth's crust broke up, many volcanoes all around the world began erupting at once. Fortunately for Noah, by the time the ark landed on the lava plateau, it had cooled and hardened.

Now that you know what was happening outside the ark, let's have a look inside to see how Noah and his family and all the animals survived the wild ride.

**5.**

# How Did They Live on the Ark?

# Noah's Family Living Space

Noah and his family most likely lived in the middle of the top deck. There they felt the rolling waves the least. The top deck was also closest to the fresh air coming in, and had the most light. They were going to be living on the ark for over a year, so they probably made their living space large and comfortable. Let's try to imagine it. We don't actually know what it was like. This is only a guess:

Maybe in the middle was their kitchen with an oven made of bricks. Beside it was a large wooden table with benches where they ate and talked.

Here is what the kitchen may have looked like: On the first wall were cupboards with many pots, pans, and knives. Underneath was a counter on which to prepare food. On the second wall were cupboards with many jars of honey, vinegar, salt, spices, and herbs. On the third wall were cupboards with flour, olives, olive oil, figs, cheeses, and nuts. On the fourth wall were containers of water for drinking and cooking.

"Only eight people were saved from drowning in that terrible flood" (1 Peter 3:20 NLT). Since Noah had a wife, and all three of their sons had wives, there were four bedrooms around the kitchen.

The bathroom was nearby. Beside it was a room with a big tub where they could wash clothes and even bathe. Close to the living quarters was a room full of wood for the oven.

# Sleepy, Hibernating Animals

At first, when all the shaking and thundering was happening outside, the animals went crazy with fear. The ark would have echoed with the noise. It must have nearly deafened Noah and his family. They probably didn't sleep much for the first few days.

Then, although the storm continued outside, God calmed the animals. Many people, when they're afraid or worried, feel sleepy. That's what God did to the animals. He caused many of them to hibernate. Animals still hibernate today. The black bear sleeps without eating for 100 days! So Noah didn't have to feed the bears for quite a while. He may even have put a sign on their cage: DO NOT FEED THE BEARS.

Marmots are rodents like

Other animals that hibernate:

- ➤ Big brown bats hibernate for 2 months.
- ➤ Hedgehogs hibernate for 4 months.
- ➤ Fat-tailed dwarf lemurs hibernate for 7 months.
- ➤ Box turtles hibernate for 5 months.
- ➤ Snails can hibernate for years.

squirrels. They hibernate for eight months. They only spend four months in summer awake, eating, and having young. Normally, their heart beats 120 times a minute. When they hibernate it slows down to just three to four times a minute. And they only take two to three breaths a minute. That's barely breathing!

Of course, many animals like elephants and hippos don't hibernate. Since God didn't want them getting excited and breaking out of their cages, He probably slowed them down to make them sleepy and calm. This was good for another reason: with most of the animals sleeping so much, they didn't eat a lot of food. And they didn't produce so much waste.

# Feeding the Animals

Even though some animals were hibernating, and most others were eating less than they normally did, there were thousands and thousands of hungry animals on the ark. And they had to be fed every day. This was a huge job. You know what that's like if it's your job to feed a cat or dog. If you forget them, they make lots of noise to remind you.

Noah could have stored all the grain and food all in one place—and then carried it halfway across the ark every time he fed every animal. That would've been lots of work. And it wouldn't have been very smart. So when God gave Noah the plans for the ark, He probably told him to build many food storage rooms on each deck. Then Noah and his sons could have fed all the creatures quicker and easier.

We know that when God designed the outside of the ark, He designed it the perfect shape and size to survive the Flood. The ark was planned by the most intelligent person in the universe—God Himself. So it makes sense that He would also have designed the inside of the ark to make things easy for Noah and his family. God not only thinks of big things, but He also thinks of all the small details.

# Watering the Animals

They needed lots of water on the ark, so Noah would have built giant water containers on all three decks. But he probably didn't put much water in them. He didn't need to. Remember, it rained for 40 days and nights at the beginning of the Flood. Water that landed on the roof of the ark could have gone into gutters and pipes that led down into the containers. The rainwater would have quickly filled all the containers on the ark.

But then how did they get water to every pen and cage? Did they carry it in buckets? They could have done that, but that would have been a lot of work. And they already had enough to do every day. They would've made endless trips. And water is heavy!

A little planning ahead of time probably saved them a lot of work. When they were building the ark, God may have inspired them to put water pipes along the outside of the animal pens. Then for the next year, they could simply have turned on taps in every pen to water the animals. They didn't need to carry thousands of buckets. They could simply have walked down the halls opening taps.

Some people wonder how Noah stored enough water on the ark to last one full year. But it probably rained several times during the following months. Yes, rain fell for the first 40 days, but that wasn't the last time it ever rained on earth. It was just the last time it ever rained so hard. So Noah probably had no problem keeping his water tanks full.

They probably had lots of water on the ark. So, yes, they probably filled ponds for the penguins, crocodiles, otters, hippos, ducks, and other beasts that like to spend lots of time in the water. And they had enough to change the water when it got dirty.

And after a long day of cleaning up stinky animal droppings, there was even enough water for Noah and his family to take baths. Thank goodness!

Rainy days per year in different places:

- Manaus, Brazil: about 176 days a year
- Seattle, Washington: about 154 days a year
- Miami, Florida: about 135 days a year
- Death Valley, California: about 14 days a year
- Atacama Desert, Chile: some parts never get rain

# Keeping the Ark Clean

Some people don't like to think about animal waste, but it's a fact of life on farms and zoos. And it was on the ark, too. Noah and his sons couldn't simply let it pile up in the pens and cages. The animals would get filthy and sick. So they had to clean it out on a regular basis—almost every day.

Now the animals' liquid waste could have drained away from their pens into ditches along the sides of the hallway. This liquid from the two upper floors could have filled huge containers on the bottom floor. The liquid from the lowest deck, however, probably drained into a space under the floor at the bottom of the ark.

Noah and sons had a big job every day cleaning out the solid waste. On the two top decks, the waste could be scooped up, carted off in wheelbarrows, and dropped into large containers on the bottom deck. But the dung on the bottom deck had to

An adult African elephant can produce up to 300 pounds of dung every day. Rhinos only create about 50 pounds of dung a day. Horses make 15 to 35 pounds a day.

be hauled up sets of stairs and dumped in bins. (By the way, that's probably where the flies lived. Flies are "unclean" animals, but they probably produced hundreds of little flies very quickly.)

When the ark landed on Mount Ararat and wasn't in the sea anymore, they could open up taps and let the liquid waste drain out of the ship through big pipes. And they could simply dump the dung out the sides. That way it didn't smell so bad inside the ark.

# An Average Day on the Ark

Just for fun, let's imagine that Noah kept a diary and that we get to look at a page. It might have said something like this:

*Today was the 160th day since the Flood began. It's also 10 days since we landed on a mountain. It's such a relief to not rock back and forth all day long. I always wondered if the next wave would tip the ark and knock me off my feet.*

*Breakfast today was milk with cereal, sprinkled with raisins. . .again. I'm beginning to wonder why we packed so many raisins.*

*Then, on to feeding the animals. As usual, we fed the birds first. They're easy. Mostly just dried fruit and grain. Four days ago, the howler monkeys escaped their cage, and they have run all over the ark since then. Ham tricked them back into their cages this morning with some figs. The box turtles finally woke up from their long hibernation—and were they ever hungry!*

*We did half the middle deck before lunch; then we stopped to eat. I was famished. We had fresh-baked bread, cheese, olives, and date cakes. I stuffed myself with olives. Then back to work. We finished the middle deck early today, probably because we gave the animals lots of water yesterday.*

*Then down to the bottom deck. I was cleaning a huge pile of waste in the rhinos' pen when I slipped and fell. I got completely filthy. That was the end of my work for a while. I went upstairs and washed up. I'm getting too old for this kind of thing.*

*Dinner was a delicious vegetable stew. Shem and I*

played a game of checkers after the meal. He won, as usual. Meanwhile Ham and Japheth played some music and their wives sang. Ham's wife has a lovely voice.

We all wonder when the world will dry up and we can finally leave the ark. I want some solid ground under my feet. Also, I'm getting very tired of raisins. I think the first thing I'll do is grow fresh grapes.

# 6.

# How Did the Flood Change the Earth?

# Mountains Rise and Oceans Sink

We already learned that the earth's crust cracked apart into seven large plates and some smaller ones. Water violently exploded up out of the cracks. It burst out with such force that it shot miles high before falling back to earth as rain. The force of all this water was so great that it pushed the plates apart. Soon the plates were moving very fast away from each other. They slid across the mantle of the earth.

Up until then, "mountains" were really only high hills. There were no Rocky Mountains or Andes or Himalayas. But as these huge plates of the earth's crust pushed apart, they began smashing into other plates. Then several different things happened:

(1) Sometimes one plate went under another plate, down into the earth. There the heat inside the planet melted it. Volcanoes often happen in places where different plates crush against each other. There are many volcanoes around the Pacific Ocean Plate.

(2) Sometimes both plates crumpled upward and formed high mountains. Instead of one plate going down, both plates pushed up. This is why some mountains are so steep and high.

(3) Sometimes plates slide past each other, like they do along the San Andreas Fault in California. This can cause big earthquakes.

As the mountains were being pushed up, the oceans were sinking. The reason is simple. The plates were moving quickly, and this created tremendous heat. The rocks under the crust melted and became soft like gelatin. This made it easier for the crust to slide over them. But it did something else, too. The crust on the ocean bottoms is heavier than the crust of the land, so the oceans sank in the soft rock.

The Bible talks about this. It says, "You [God] clothed the earth with floods of water, water that covered even the mountains. At your command, the water fled. . .it hurried away. Mountains rose and valleys sank" (Psalm 104:6–8 NLT).

# Sedimentary Rocks and Fossils

As you learn in school, there are three types of rocks on earth: igneous rocks, metamorphic rocks, and sedimentary rocks. When lava comes out of volcanoes then cools and hardens, it forms igneous rocks. *Metamorphosis* means "change," so metamorphic rocks are rocks that go through a huge change because of heat and pressure.

But what we're interested in here are sedimentary rocks. First, rocks are crushed into very fine grains. When water is moving fast, these grains float. When the water slows down, these sediments settle on the bottom. Some sedimentary rocks are chalk, sandstone, limestone, and clay. In places they are hundreds of feet deep—and they cover about 75 percent of the planet! This was caused by the Flood.

All fossils of ancient plants and animals are found in sedimentary rocks. How did this happen? Well, as the superhot, high-pressure water from "the fountains of the deep" exploded out of the cracks, it wore away the sides of the plates. It turned them into fine grains. These grains fell back to the earth with the rain. They filled the water as clouds of mud. They settled on all the animals and plants that drowned in the Flood. They covered and buried them.

Then, over many centuries, the mud hardened into sedimentary rocks. The plants and animals turned into stone and became fossils. Some parts of the world are full of fossils.

In some places, huge amounts of fossils are jumbled together in "fossil beds." Why is this? When the Flood hit the earth, billions of tons of water rushed across the land and swept away the animals. It dumped them in valleys where they sank. Then they were all covered with mud. That's why they're all lumped together.

Here are some famous fossils people found:

- Megalosaurus (discovered 1676)

- Mosasaurus (discovered 1764)

- Iguanodon (discovered 1820)

- Hadrosaurus (discovered 1858)

- Archaeopteryx (discovered 1860)

# Coal, Oil, and Gas

There was no coal, oil, or natural gas in the earth before the Flood. They were all created during it.

Here's how coal formed: Before the Flood, there were huge forests with trees and giant ferns 100 feet tall. And there were swamps filled with normal-sized ferns. When tidal waves swept over the land, they smashed down millions of trees—flattening entire forests—and swept them into valleys. They also covered the swamps. Because there was no oxygen at the bottom of all that water, the plants didn't rot right away.

Then sediments settled over them. Tons and tons of sediments covered these buried forests. The sediments turned into sedimentary rocks. All their weight created great pressure. This squeezed the water out of the plants. And the pressure also created heat. The pressure and heat turned the vegetation into coal.

These countries have the most coal: (1) the United States, (2) Russia, (3) China, (4) India, and (5) Australia. That means they once had the greatest fern forests on earth.

Here's how oil and natural gas formed: Billions

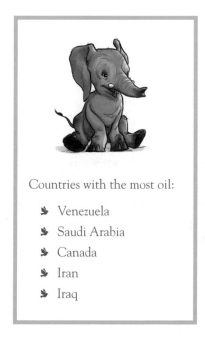

Countries with the most oil:

- Venezuela
- Saudi Arabia
- Canada
- Iran
- Iraq

and billions of animals died in the Flood. Most of them didn't turn into hard fossils like rock. Instead, they were swept together and crushed under tons of sedimentary rocks. Their body juices turned into natural gas and oil.

There are also large lakes of oil under the rocks at the bottom of oceans. That's why there are oil rigs out in the Gulf of Mexico. Billions of animals were swept out to sea and sank to the bottom. There they were crushed under millions of tons of sediments. This turned them into oil.

# The Grand Canyon

The Grand Canyon of Arizona is made of sedimentary rocks that settled during the Flood. Many people believe that the Grand Canyon was carved as the water was draining off the continents after the Deluge. But this is not what happened. Instead, there was probably a huge lake left in the area from the floodwaters. Sometime after the Flood, the southern banks of this lake broke. All the water roared toward the sea, carving the Grand Canyon. This happened very quickly. It didn't take millions of years.

# The Ice Age and Glaciers

Earlier we learned that when the earth's crust broke apart, volcanoes began erupting all over the world. Billions of tons of ash went into the atmosphere. The sky became so dark that the sun couldn't shine on the ground. This made the earth very cold. Much of the water that sprayed high into the cold atmosphere fell to earth as ice crystals or snow.

Remember, the sea was very warm because of the heat of the moving crust. When the world was still flooded, the snow melted in the water. But after a while, the water level went down and dry land appeared. There were great blizzards. Snow began piling up at the North and South Poles. Soon great ice caps covered the poles. Christian experts say that glaciers grew for 500 years until ice covered one-third of the earth. The Ice Age had begun!

Mammoths and other animals with

In August 1883, a huge volcano called Krakatoa exploded. The roar was so loud that people heard it nearly 2,000 miles away. It sent so much ash into the air that the entire earth was colder for five years.

long, warm hair moved north into the cold northern lands. They usually kept warm. But the weather was so bad that sometimes terrific blizzards swept over them. This froze them right away. That's why scientists sometimes dig mammoths out of the frozen ground, and their bodies haven't rotted at all.

Some cool Ice Age animals:

- woolly mammoth
- wooly rhinoceros
- saber-toothed tiger
- giant hyena
- giant ground sloth

After another 200 years, the world's temperature began to rise again. Slowly the great glaciers began melting and shrinking. Every year the glaciers melted back another 30 feet. But ice still covers the North Pole and the continent of Antarctica, on the bottom of the world.

# 7.

# What Happened after the Flood?

# The Mountains of Ararat

The Bible says, "The ark came to rest on the mountains of Ararat" (Genesis 8:4 NIV). Many people think this means that the ark landed on the very top of Mount Ararat. It didn't. But they think that Ararat is just one mountain, so that's where the ark had to land. But the Bible says, "The ark came to rest on the mountains of Ararat." Notice that it says "mountains."

Ararat is a huge volcanic mound 25 miles across. Two steep peaks rise up from this mound. There are many miles between these two mountains. Yet the Bible says the ark landed on "the mountains of Ararat." How could the ark be on both mountains at once? Simple. The ark probably landed in a lower spot on the volcanic mound between the two mountains. Most people have looked for the ark high on the tallest peak. No wonder they didn't find it. They were probably looking in the wrong place.

Also, Mount Ararat's tallest peak is very steep. If the ark landed up

The two mountain peaks of "the mountains of Ararat" are Greater Ararat (16,854 feet high) and Lesser Ararat (12,782 feet high).

there, how did all the animals climb down after they left the ship? The nimble goats could have done it. But most animals wouldn't have made it.

# Plants Fill the Earth Again

Some people wonder where all the plants came from after the Flood. After all, God didn't tell Noah to take plants on the ark, did He? And during the Flood, tidal waves wiped out earth's forests, buried them under hundreds of feet of mud, and turned them into coal.

Yet, one day, when Noah sent out a dove, she came back with an olive leaf in her beak (Genesis 8:11). So at least one olive tree was growing on earth! How did it survive? First of all, billions of trees were uprooted by the rushing waters of the Flood. Most were buried by mud underwater. But some floated on the surface of the ocean. At times they even lumped together in big floating islands.

Many seeds became soaked with water and rotted. But an olive seed (called a "pit") is hard. So after the Deluge, the olive pit ended up on the earth again. Then it sprouted and grew.

But guess what?

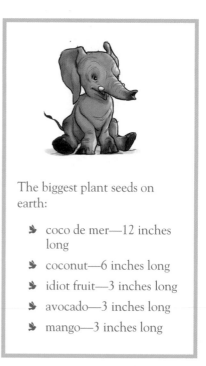

The biggest plant seeds on earth:

- ❧ coco de mer—12 inches long
- ❧ coconut—6 inches long
- ❧ idiot fruit—3 inches long
- ❧ avocado—3 inches long
- ❧ mango—3 inches long

Olive trees would have been around after the Flood even if one hadn't survived out in the storm. Why? Because Noah took vases of olives on board the ark for food, and olives all have seeds. They had lots and lots of olive seeds to plant.

They also had seeds of many other trees, plants, and grains. God told Noah, "You are to take every kind of food that is to be eaten and store it away" (Genesis 6:21 NIV). So Noah would have stored huge clay jars full of every kind of fruit, vegetable, herb, nut, berry, and grain. The fruits, vegetables, and berries were dried first. And the "fruit" of all these plants have seeds inside.

In fact, although the Bible doesn't tell us, Noah had 120 years to gather seeds from every kind of tree on earth. He could easily have done it—even as a hobby on the side. Some people collect stamps or coins. Noah could have collected plant seeds. After all, Johnny Appleseed spent 46 years collecting and planting apple seeds. Even Abraham planted a tree (Genesis 21:33). We should give Noah credit for a few good ideas!

The largest seed in the world is the coco de mer, the seed of a palm tree. Some are 12 inches long and weigh up to 40 pounds. That's just one seed!

# Letting the Animals Go

When the earth was finally dry, and plants were growing all over again, God told Noah, "Come out of the ark, you and your wife and your sons and their wives. Bring out every kind of living creature that is with you" (Genesis 8:16–17 NIV).

Let's think about how Noah did this. His family probably opened the birdcages on the upper deck first. And the birds likely flew straight out the nearest window. They let out all the seed-eating, insect-eating birds before the hawks, eagles, and owls. Best to give the little guys a head start!

Then Noah and his sons removed the heavy wooden bars from the door and opened it. They opened most of the cages on the middle deck. They probably let out the deer, antelope, ostriches, warthogs, and all the other plant-eating creatures first. "Everything. . .came out of the ark, one kind after another" (Genesis 8:19 NIrV).

Then they opened all the cages and pens on the bottom deck, letting out the elephants, mammoths, hippos, and large plant-eating dinosaurs. But remember: The dinosaurs weren't so large yet. They still had years of growing to do.

They waited until all these animals were safely out of sight. Then Noah and his sons went back to the middle deck of the ark and opened the cages of the wolves, cheetahs, lions, and saber-toothed tigers. Then, and only then, they went to the lower deck and very carefully set the two T. rexes free.

# God's Rainbow Promise

One thing Noah and his family noticed right away was that the weather was cool outside the ark. Remember, the Ice Age was starting. Besides, they were high up on a lava mound near the two mountains of Ararat.

"Then Noah built an altar to honor the LORD. He took some of all of the 'clean' animals and birds. He sacrificed them on the altar as burnt offerings" (Genesis 8:20 NIrV). Since there were many, many "clean" animals and birds, Noah must have sacrificed hundreds of them. They didn't eat the meat, either. They burned them up completely. That's what people did to "burnt offerings."

After that, God made a promise: "I will never again destroy all living things. . . . Never again will a flood destroy the earth" (Genesis 8:21; 9:11 NLT). Then God made a beautiful sign in the sky and said, "Here is the sign of

Seven colors in a rainbow:

- ❧ red
- ❧ orange
- ❧ yellow
- ❧ green
- ❧ blue
- ❧ indigo
- ❧ violet

the covenant I am making. I have put my rainbow in the clouds" (Genesis 9:12–13 NIrv).

However, this rainbow that Noah and his family saw wasn't from the Flood. Remember, it had stopped raining at the end of the 40 days—and that was nearly a year ago! So God must have sent a short shower just after Noah finished his sacrifices.

## Wild Animals and Livestock

There were seven of each "clean" animal on the ark. But after Noah sacrificed one of each "clean" animal, there were only six left. Now here's something interesting: There were still six sheep, six goats, and six cattle. Noah probably released a pair of each of these into the wild, but he kept some with him. He needed them for meat and milk. God talked about bringing "wild animals and livestock" (Genesis 8:1 NIrV) on the ark. *Livestock* means tame farm animals. That means that some animals were tame before the Flood.

In the book of Job, God asks, "Who let the wild donkey go free? Who untied its ropes?" (Job 39:5 NIV). In Job's day, people had tame donkeys that worked hard, carrying heavy loads. But there were also wild donkeys running around, doing

Originally, there were no rabbits in Australia. But people brought tame rabbits there, and some escaped. Soon there were millions of wild rabbits. Rabbits caused problems and ate crops in Australia, so people built the Rabbit-Proof Fence to keep them out of western farmlands. It was 2,000 miles long. But it didn't really work.

nothing. People wondered where the wild donkeys came from. Noah probably kept donkeys with him after the Flood. But years later, some escaped into the wild and ran around.

This happened with horses, too. Horses were originally wild. Then people captured some and tamed them. They used them to ride on and pull chariots. Many centuries later, Europeans brought horses to North America. But some of them escaped. They became known as mustangs.

# Animals Fill the Earth Again

At the very beginning of Creation, God had blessed the animals and commanded them to multiply. For example, He said to the sea creatures and birds, "Be fruitful and increase in number and fill the water in the seas, and let the birds increase on the earth" (Genesis 1:22 NIV).

The Flood destroyed almost every animal on earth. "But God showed concern for Noah. He also showed concern for all of the wild animals and livestock that were with Noah in the ark" (Genesis 8:1 NIrV). After the Flood, God made a promise to both people and animals: "When I see the rainbow in the clouds, I will remember the eternal covenant between God and every living creature on earth" (Genesis 9:16 NLT).

Once again it was God's will that the animals "increase in number." So He told Noah, "Bring out every kind of living thing that is with you. Bring the birds, the animals, and all of the creatures that move along the ground. Then they can multiply on the earth. They can have little ones and the number of

There were enormous dragonflies before the Flood. People have found dragonfly fossils that were 6 feet wide from wing tip to wing tip. But these creatures all died out.

them can increase" (Genesis 8:17 NIrv).

With so much of the world's water frozen in great glaciers, the sea level was about 400 feet lower during the Ice Age than it is today. So even though North America was now a separate continent, there was a land bridge between it and Asia. So the animals could cross from Asia to America. And they did. They also made their way down to Australia over land bridges.

Some animals didn't increase very much. The new earth was colder than the ancient world, and most dinosaurs didn't do well in the new climate. Some of their favorite plants weren't around anymore. Soon they died out completely. Other animals, like saber-toothed tigers, mammoths, and Brontotheres, lasted longer. Then they died out centuries later. Animals are still dying in the world today. When there are no more of a certain kind of animal, scientists say that it has become "extinct."

Modern animals that have become extinct:

- the 850-pound elephant bird (1700s)
- the dodo bird (1662)
- the quagga, a kind of zebra (1883)
- the passenger pigeon (1914)
- the Tasmanian tiger (1936)

# People Live Shorter Lives

Before the Flood, people sometimes lived over 900 years. Methuselah lived to be 969. But after the Flood, people didn't live as long.

Some Christians think that the earth's magnetic field was not as strong. Or they think that the water canopy had fallen. These things no longer blocked all the harmful rays from the sun, so people began living shorter and shorter lives. These may have been part of the reason. But these were not the full reason. After all, Noah was 600 years old when the Flood hit. And he lived 350 years after the Flood. So he lived 950 years in all.

The reason people no longer live for centuries may be that this is simply what God decided. Our bodies are made up of billions of tiny cells. Inside the cells are even tinier things called DNA. This DNA has instructions that say whether we will have blue eyes or

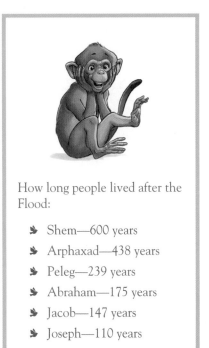

How long people lived after the Flood:

- Shem—600 years
- Arphaxad—438 years
- Peleg—239 years
- Abraham—175 years
- Jacob—147 years
- Joseph—110 years

brown eyes. It has instructions that say how long we will live. Many instructions can be switched off and on—just like a light switch. Before the Flood, God switched "on" the instructions for long life. But after the Flood, God switched long life to "off." He didn't want people to live over 900 years anymore.

# The Story Lives On

Noah and his family didn't move far from Mount Ararat for many years. They probably built farmhouses in a warm, well-watered valley below the mountain. There they raised cattle, sheep, and goats. They plowed the land and planted grain fields and gardens. "After the flood, Noah began to cultivate the ground, and he planted a vineyard" (Genesis 9:20 NLT).

Noah's sons began having children, and soon there were little kids running all over the place. Then they grew up and they had children, too. After a while, there were hundreds and hundreds of people on the earth. Noah lived to be very old. "Noah lived another 350 years after the great flood" (Genesis 9:28 NLT). He had many great-great-great-great-great-grandchildren. And just like children today, they loved to hear the story of Noah's ark. They could have heard it from Noah himself.

Everyone on earth heard the story about

Mount Ararat is right next to the modern countries of Armenia and Georgia. Experts tell us that these are the first places on earth where people planted vineyards and made wine. Why is that? Because Noah had been there!

a great hero saving all the people and animals from the great Flood. That's why in many countries around the world, people still tell stories about it. Native tribes in North and South America have legends about a great flood. So do tribes all over Africa. Even the Aborigines of Australia tell tales about a mighty Deluge. People from Asia to Europe to the Pacific Islands have very old Flood stories. They've changed many details, but the main part of the story is the same.

# The Search to Find the Ark

Mount Ararat is in a very dangerous part of the world. The local people are called Kurds, and they often have gun battles with government soldiers near Mount Ararat. Sometimes they shoot at people who come looking for Noah's ark.

Also, Mount Ararat is a volcano. The last time it erupted was in 1840. There is great danger from earthquakes, rock slides, and mud slides. At the top of the mountain where there's snow, there are often avalanches. There are also wild storms, lightning, and thick fog. Several explorers have fallen into deep cracks on the sides of the mountain and died.

A number of people claim that they have found the ark on Mount Ararat. But when others ask to see the ark, those people can never find it again. This leads us to wonder whether anyone has really found the ark at all.

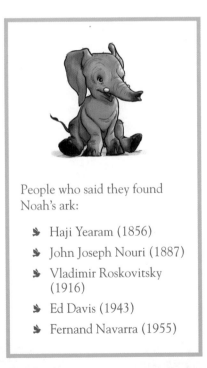

People who said they found Noah's ark:

- Haji Yearam (1856)
- John Joseph Nouri (1887)
- Vladimir Roskovitsky (1916)
- Ed Davis (1943)
- Fernand Navarra (1955)

So far, no one has ever brought back proof that they found the ark. Some people show pieces of wood and say it came from Noah's ark. But so far all the wood has not been very old. It has been from something else, not the ark. Sometimes people say they have photographs of things that look like the ark. But they turn out to be just lumps of rocks.

So where is the ark? Maybe it landed in a different part of the mountains of Ararat. Maybe people can't find it because they're looking in the wrong place. Perhaps the ark is also covered with mud and rocks. It would be very exciting to find it one day, but no one has found it yet.

# Noah and the End Times

The Bible says, "God did not spare the ancient world—except for Noah and the seven others in his family. Noah warned the world of God's righteous judgment. So God protected Noah when he destroyed the world of ungodly people with a vast flood" (2 Peter 2:5 NLT).

God promised to never again destroy the world with a flood. But one day, after Jesus returns, God will judge the world again. This time, He will destroy the world with a mighty earthquake and monstrous hailstones (Revelation 16:18–21). After that, He will burn the earth with fire (2 Peter 3:10). Then He will make a beautiful new world for His people to live on forever (Isaiah 65:17; Revelation 21:1).

When will this happen? Jesus called Himself "the Son of Man," and He said, "When the Son of Man returns, it will be like it was in Noah's day. In those days before the flood, the people were enjoying banquets and parties and weddings right up to the time Noah entered his boat. People didn't realize what was going to happen until the flood came and swept them all away. That is the way it will be when the Son of Man comes" (Matthew 24:37–39 NLT).

Are you ready for Jesus to return? If you believe in God's Son and love Him, then when He comes back, He will take you to heaven in the Rapture. After that, God will judge the world. But you and all the other people who love Jesus will be safe—just like Noah and his family were safe inside the ark. After God has finished judging the earth, He will make the whole world into a paradise like the Garden of Eden. That will be our forever home. See you there!

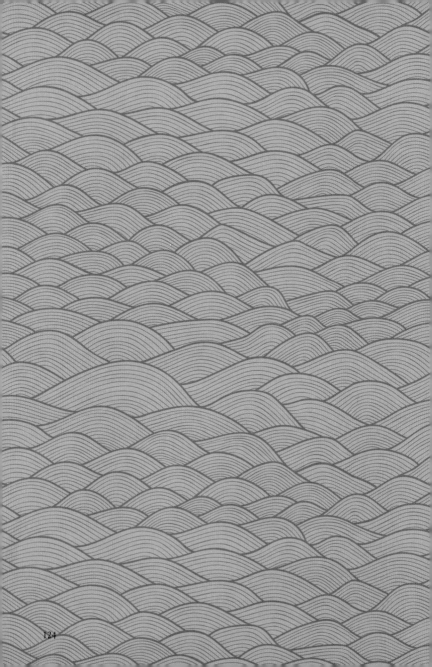

# Scripture Index

# Old Testament

# New Testament